bubblefacts...

PLANET EARTH

MILES KELLY

PUBLISHING

First published in 2005 by
Miles Kelly Publishing Ltd
Bardfield Centre, Great Bardfield, Essex, CM7 4SL

2 4 6 8 10 9 7 5 3 1

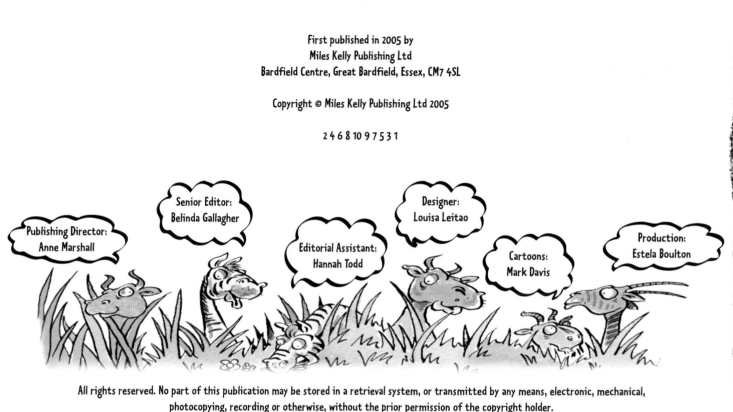

Publishing Director:
Anne Marshall

Senior Editor:
Belinda Gallagher

Editorial Assistant:
Hannah Todd

Designer:
Louisa Leitao

Cartoons:
Mark Davis

Production:
Estela Boulton

ISBN 1-84236-521-5

Printed in China

British Library Cataloguing-in-Publication Data
A catalogue record for this book is available from the British Library

Indexer: Jane Parker

www.mileskelly.net
info@mileskelly.net

Contents

HOW was Earth born?

baby planet

The Earth came from a cloud in space. Scientists think that the Earth formed from a huge cloud of gas and dust around 4500 million years ago. A star near the cloud exploded, making it spin. As the cloud spun around, gases gathered at its centre and formed the Sun.

Dust whizzed around the Sun and stuck together to form rocks that eventually became the planets.

The new Earth was very hot. Volcanoes erupted, releasing steam and gas. As the Earth cooled, the steam changed to water droplets and made clouds. Eventually, rain fell from the clouds. Over millions of years, this rain made the seas and oceans.

Millions of rocks crash into Earth as it speeds through space. Some larger ones may reach the ground as meteorites.

Rocks called meteorites crashed into the Earth and Moon, making hollows called craters.

Earth in a spin

getting dizzy!

The Earth is like a huge spinning top. It keeps spinning because it was formed from a whirling cloud of gas and dust. Instead of spinning straight up like a top, the Earth leans a little to one side and takes 24 hours to turn around once. This period of time is called a day.

FAR OUT MAN!

IT'S DAYTIME, TIME TO WAKE UP.

TZZZZ!

TZZZZ!

The Earth travels around the Sun as it spins. This is called its orbit and it takes a year to complete.

The spinning Earth acts like a magnet. At the centre of the Earth is liquid iron. As the Earth spins, it makes the iron behave like a magnet with a North and South Pole. These act on the magnet in a compass to make the needle point to the North and South.

The Earth spins around two points at opposite ends of its surface. One is on top of the Earth and is called the North Pole. The other is at the bottom of the Earth and is called the South Pole. The North and South Poles are covered in snow and ice.

The Earth's spinning makes day and night. When a part of the Earth faces the Sun it is daytime.

Hot, hot rocks...
and boiling lava

Volcanoes are places where hot, liquid rock shoots up through the Earth's surface. Beneath a volcano is a huge chamber called the magma chamber, filled with molten (liquid) rock. Inside, pressure builds. Eventually ash, steam and molten rock called lava escape from the top of the volcano – this is an eruption.

The crust of the Earth is broken up into plates. These can move very slightly and create volcanoes.

There are volcanoes under the sea. Where plates in the Earth's crust move apart, lava flows out from a volcano to fill the gap. The hot lava is cooled quickly by the sea and forms pillow-shaped lumps called pillow lava.

Some creatures that die are preserved in rocks - we call these fossils. Some fossils of bacteria are three and a half billion years old.

Volcanoes can erupt in different ways - some have runny lava and some have thick lava.

Boil and bubble
steam cleaning!

Geysers can be found on top of some volcanoes. If a volcano collapses, its rocks settle above hot rocks in its magma chamber. Rainwater seeps into gaps between the rocks, collecting in the chamber, where it is heated until it boils. A build up of steam then pushes a big spurt of water high into the air.

Steam and fumes can escape from holes called fumaroles. Ancient Romans used them as steam baths.

Some mud pots are cool enough to wallow in. As the bubbles in a mud pot grow, they pop, and fumes escape into the air. Wallowing in a mud pot can make your skin soft and smooth.

Millions of years ago, plants died, fell into swamps and did not rot. Their remains were squashed and heated so much that they turned into coal.

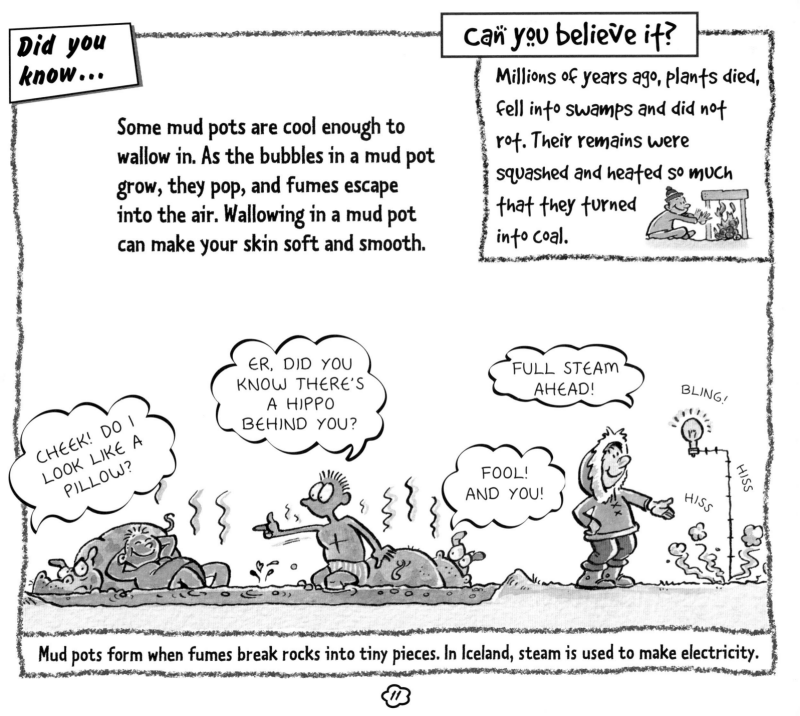

Mud pots form when fumes break rocks into tiny pieces. In Iceland, steam is used to make electricity.

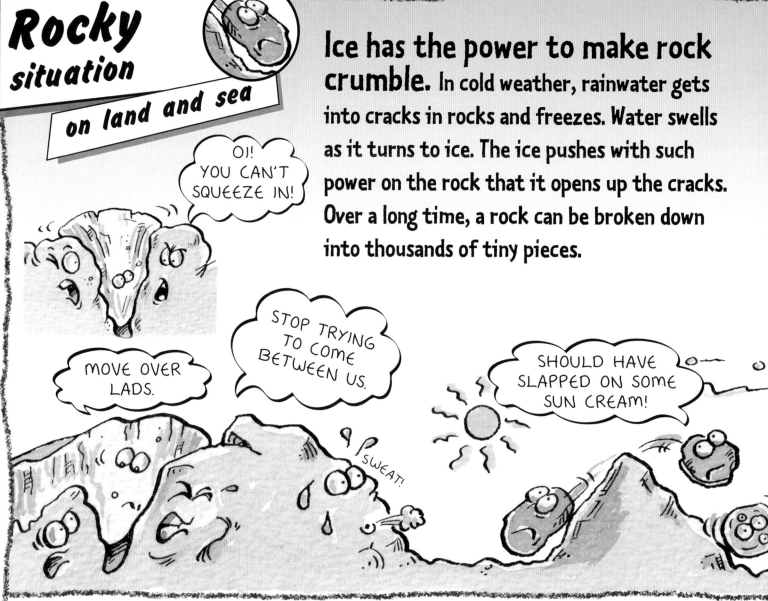

Rocky situation on land and sea

Ice has the power to make rock crumble. In cold weather, rainwater gets into cracks in rocks and freezes. Water swells as it turns to ice. The ice pushes with such power on the rock that it opens up the cracks. Over a long time, a rock can be broken down into thousands of tiny pieces.

When a rock warms up it swells, and when it cools it shrinks. Over time these actions crumble it away.

can you believe it?

In one part of Turkey, people have cut caves in huge cones of rock to make homes.

Strong winds in deserts hurl dust and sand grains at rock, which slowly blast pieces from its surface. They then blow away any tiny loose chips that have formed on the surface of the rock. Over time, this can make rocks disappear, or form strange shapes.

CHIP...

OFF THE OLD BLOCK!

OOPS! SORRY TO BREAK THINGS UP!

Rabbits can break up rock as they burrow. Glaciers are sheets of sliding ice that can break up rock.

Making rocks

settling down

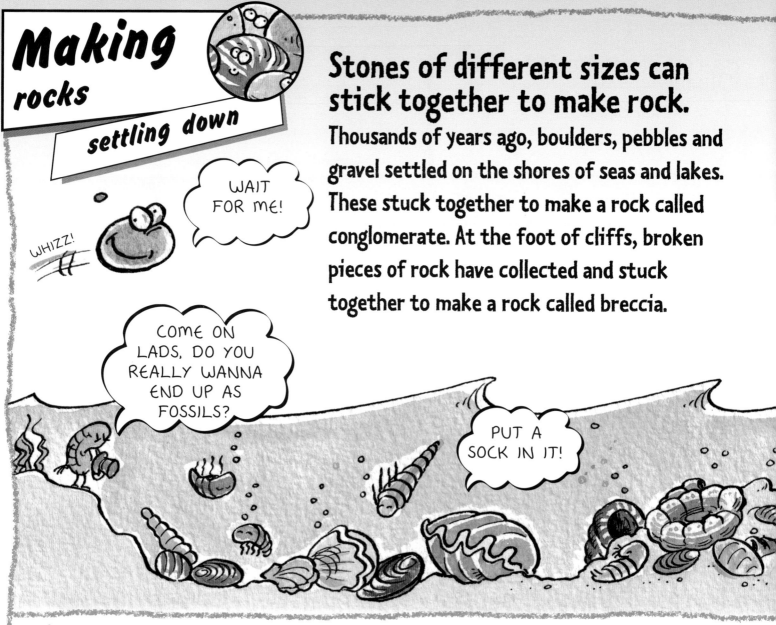

Stones of different sizes can stick together to make rock. Thousands of years ago, boulders, pebbles and gravel settled on the shores of seas and lakes. These stuck together to make a rock called conglomerate. At the foot of cliffs, broken pieces of rock have collected and stuck together to make a rock called breccia.

WHIZZ!

WAIT FOR ME!

COME ON LADS, DO YOU REALLY WANNA END UP AS FOSSILS?

PUT A SOCK IN IT!

Limestone is made from sea shells. Over time, huge numbers of shells build up and press together.

Sandstone can be made in the sea or in the desert. When a thick layer of sand builds up, the grains are pushed together and cement forms. This sticks the grains together to make sandstone. Sea sandstone can be bright yellow. Desert sandstone can be red.

WISH I'D BROUGHT MY SURF BOARD!

WHOOSH!

WHY ARE WE WAITING... WHY ARE WE WAITING?

GULP!

WIBBLE

WOBBLE

When layers of mud formed in ancient seas, they were squashed by their own weight to make mudstone.

Massive mountains

pointy peaks

The youngest mountains are the highest on Earth. The highest of all is Mount Everest, which formed 15 million years ago. Young mountains have jagged peaks because softer rocks on the mountain top are broken down by the weather. These pointy peaks are made from harder rocks that take longer to break down.

When plates in the Earth's crust crash together they crumple and fold to form mountains.

Some of Earth's highest mountains are volcanoes. With every eruption another layer of rock is added.

Block mountains are pushed up through cracks in the Earth's crust.

Beautiful crystals can grow in lava bubbles. Lava contains gases that form bubbles. When the lava cools and becomes solid, the bubbles form balloon-shaped spaces in the rock. These are called geodes. Liquids seep into them and form large crystals. The gemstone amethyst forms in this way.

I DON'T WANNA BE A CARAT!

OKAY, I GIVE IN!

WE'RE THE BIGGEST ROCKS ROUND HERE!

GOOD!

EEK!

Gemstones are beautiful coloured rocks. They can be cut and polished to make them sparkle.

Gold forms as small grains or nuggets in rocks. When the rock wears away the grains are exposed.

Emeralds and diamonds are used to make jewellery. Diamond is the hardest substance on Earth.

pitter patter!

The Earth is wrapped in layers of gases called the atmosphere. The weather takes place in the lowest layer, the troposphere. The layer above is the stratosphere. Aeroplanes fly here to avoid bad weather. The mesosphere is the middle layer, and above it is the thermosphere. The exosphere is 700 kilometres above your head.

MORNING, SUNSHINE!

A BIT OF A SQUEEZE...

SIZZLE!

MOVE IT, PUFFY!

JUST DROPPING BY!

GRR!

SPLISH! SPLASH!

As the Sun shines on the oceans' surface, water vapour rises into the air, cools and forms rain clouds.

Every day there are 45,000 thunderstorms on Earth. A single storm can generate the same energy as a hydrogen bomb!

Snowflakes form in the very tops of clouds. It is so cold here that water freezes to make ice crystals. As the snowflakes get larger, they fall through the cloud. If the cloud is in warm air, the snowflakes melt and form raindrops. If the cloud is in cold air, snowflakes reach the ground and may settle.

CAREFUL, BOYS, FULL-SCALE TWISTER AHEAD!

LET'S TWIST AGAIN!

EEK!

I'D RATHER NOT!

Tornadoes are the fastest winds, and they form when very warm air rises quickly from the ground.

Splitting the Earth

'quake shake

Violent movements in the Earth's crust cause earthquakes. They start deep underground at a focus. Shock waves move from the focus in all directions, shaking the rock. Where the waves reach the surface is where the greatest shaking occurs. This is the epicentre.

Buildings collapse

Shock waves from the focus

The Richter Scale measures the strength of the shock waves and energy produced by an earthquake.

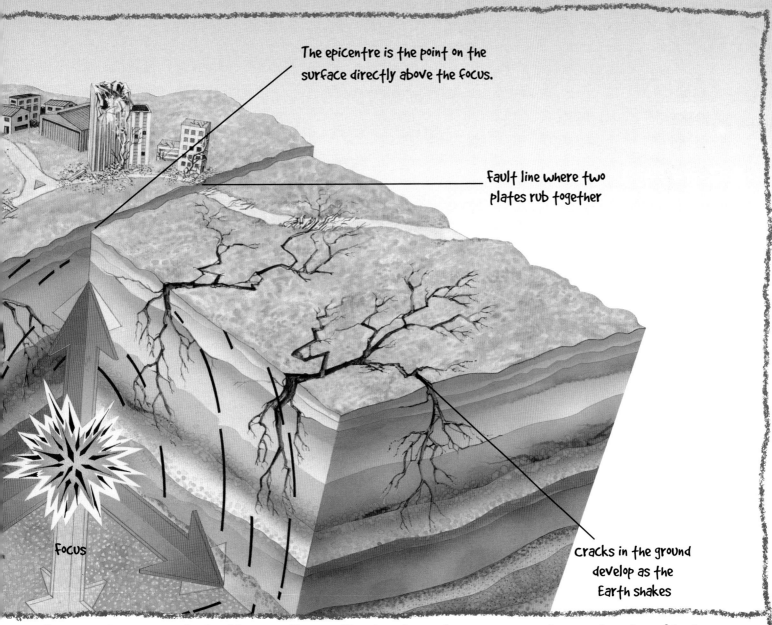

The epicentre is the point on the surface directly above the focus.

fault line where two plates rub together

focus

cracks in the ground develop as the Earth shakes

Earthquakes can make buildings collapse. Fire is a hazard too as gas mains can break and leak.

Deep in the forest
tree power!

There are three main kinds of forest – coniferous, temperate and tropical. Coniferous trees form huge forests around the northern part of the planet. They have long, green, needle-like leaves covered in wax. These trees stay in leaf throughout the year.

CHILL OUT MAN!

FLUTTER LIKE A BUTTERFLY!

YESSS?

EEEEK!

THOUGHT WE WERE PLAYING HIDE AND SEEK?

ZZZ!

Rainforests trees have broad leaves that form a roof over the forest called a canopy.

can you believe it?

Animals adapt to their surroundings. Camels have broad feet to stop them from sinking into the ground.

Coniferous trees produce seeds that are eaten by squirrels. Deer, rabbits, foxes and mice live in temperate forests. Rainforests are home to huge hairy spiders, brightly coloured frogs and spotted jungle cats.

Three-quarters of all known species of animals and plants live in rainforests.

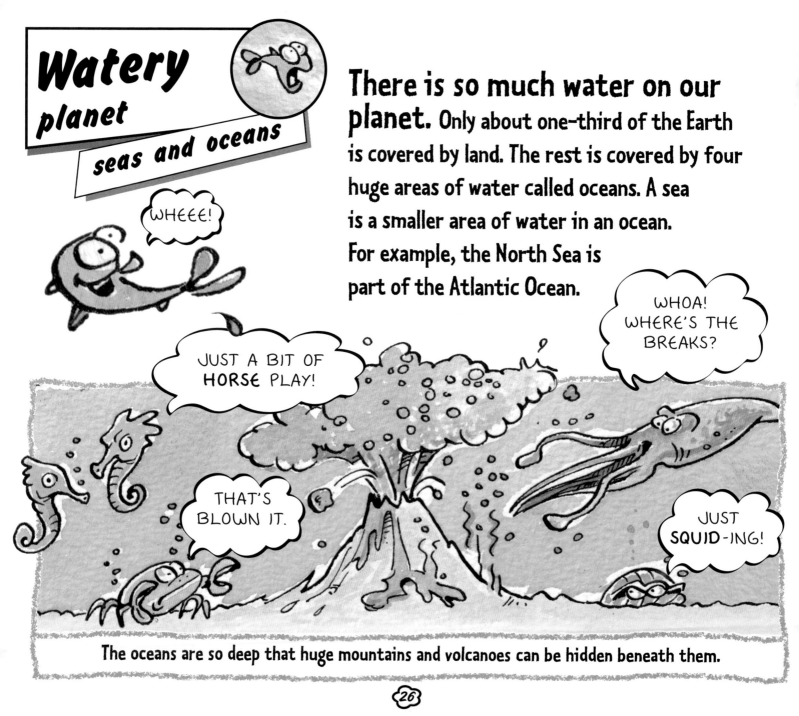

Watery planet

seas and oceans

There is so much water on our planet. Only about one-third of the Earth is covered by land. The rest is covered by four huge areas of water called oceans. A sea is a smaller area of water in an ocean. For example, the North Sea is part of the Atlantic Ocean.

WHEEE!

JUST A BIT OF HORSE PLAY!

THAT'S BLOWN IT.

WHOA! WHERE'S THE BREAKS?

JUST SQUID-ING!

The oceans are so deep that huge mountains and volcanoes can be hidden beneath them.

A river changes as it flows to the sea. It begins in mountains where it flows quickly. On flatter ground it becomes wider and slow-moving. Where the river meets the sea is called the river mouth. It may be a wide channel called an estuary or a group of sandy islands, called a delta.

Many plants and animals live in the ocean. At the North and South Poles, icebergs float in the water.

Planet of life

living it up!

There are millions of different kinds of life forms on Earth. So far, life has not been found anywhere else in the Universe. Living things survive on Earth because it is warm, there is water and the air contains oxygen. If we discover other planets with these conditions, there may be life on them, too.

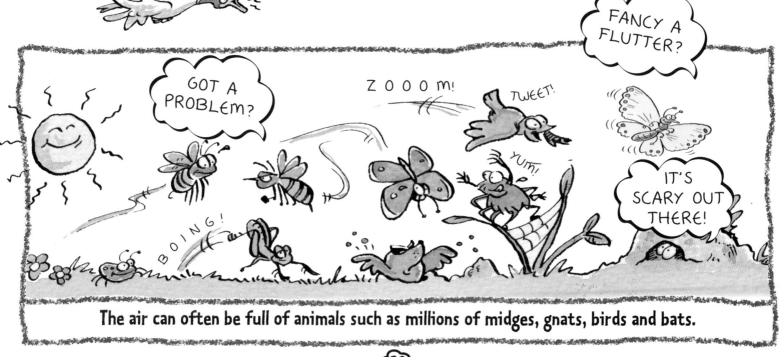

The air can often be full of animals such as millions of midges, gnats, birds and bats.

Animals cannot live without plants. Plants makes food from sunlight, water, air and minerals in the soil. Animals cannot make their own food so many of them eat plants. Others survive by eating the plant-eaters. If plants died out, animals would die too.

The star-nosed mole has feelers on the end of its nose. It uses them to find food.

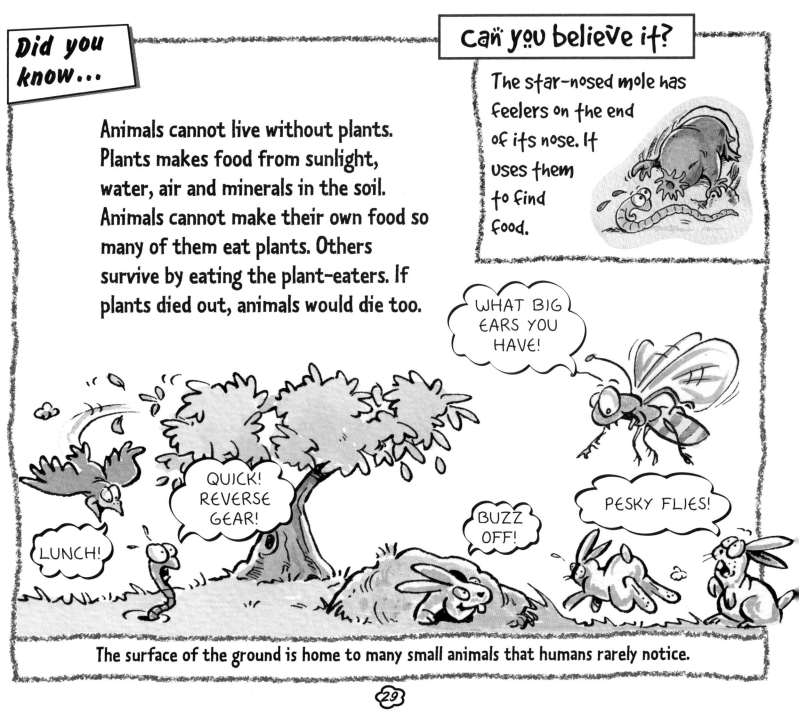

The surface of the ground is home to many small animals that humans rarely notice.

Caring for Earth

Many useful materials come from the Earth. They make clothes, buildings, furniture and containers such as cans. Some materials, such as those used to make buildings, last a long time. Others, such as those used to make cans, may be used up on the day they are bought.

IS THAT MY TUMMY RUMBLING?

LUNCH ANYONE?

A DOGGY BAG TO TAKE HOME.

In the future, we may run out of useful materials such as metal and wood.

It is important to recycle materials by sending them back to factories to be used again.

Areas of land have been made into national parks to protect wildlife and plants.

Index